LIKE US

Eme-Lou and Zeb, 1990. Spider monkey, female, 1 year old; and Chihuahua dog, male, 3 years old.

Like Us

PRIMATE PORTRAITS

ROBIN SCHWARTZ

W. W. Norton & Company
New York London

To Paul, Whitey, and Robert,
and to all the primates who have enriched my life,
especially Congo, Vana, Pete, Minnie, and Milt.

Designed and typeset by Katy Homans
Manufacturing in Italy by Arnoldo Mondadori Editore, Verona

Library of Congress Cataloging-in-Publication Data
Schwartz, Robin
Like us : primate portyraits / photographs by Robin Schwartz.
p. cm.
1. Photography of primates. I. Title.
TR729. P74S35 1993
779' .32—dc20
93-12091

ISBN 0-393-03499-2 (cl)
ISBN 0-393-31044-2 (pa)

W. W. Norton & Company, Inc. 500 Fifth Avenue, New York, N. Y. 10110
W. W. Norton & Company Ltd., 10 Coptic Street, London WC1A 1PU

1 2 3 4 5 6 7 8 9 0

ACKNOWLEDGMENTS

There are many people and animals who have helped me make the primate portrait series. I could not have made these photographs without the cooperation and trust of all the primate caretakers who allowed me into their lives, patiently giving of their time and energy, assisting me in making the photographs.

I want to thank those who graciously offered me lodging throughout my travels as well as acquainted me with primates: Lu and John Hall, Laurie Strykul, Judy Rettig, Pat Robinson, Karen Moffat, Nancy and Herb S., and Evone Finser.

I thank those who shared their experiences with primates: Joan Ballassi, Alison Pascoc, Alex Frasier, Shivani and Dhurjati Mueller, Kathy Travers, Jane Bicks and James Rapp, Maryann Milstein, Rossane D'Ercole, Mae Noell and her assistant, Julie, Connie Braun, Marilyn and Mike Sheehan, Bryce Marsh, Vicki Strawn, Toccoa and Doug Renoud, Judy Foisy, Jody Adams, Lynn Steffan, Mary Overton, Vernell Stock, Lynn Venditti, Bethany Craighead, Suzanne and Cathy Davidson, Mr. and Mrs. Bradley Hale, Deborah and Arthur, Margie Hand, Kathy Pettey, Leroy Hoover, Peg Maretta, Clayton Miller, Sue Hendricks, Carol and Jim Steele, Duke and Briggie Lee, Carol Schottlekotte,

Dawn Strasser, Julie Easton, Roberta Herman, Jan Jordan, Diane Weston, Cheryl Giacinto, Diane Brzeski, C. J. McCaffrey, and the many others who helped me find my primate subjects. I thank Pierce Onthank for introducing me to his wooleys.

I wish to offer a special thanks to Jayne Paulette, editor of the Simian Society of America Newsletter, for uniting people who care about and for primates, for publishing my simian spotlight column, and for kind encouragement and support given during many late night phone calls.

I thank Dr. Mohoney, Emily Hahn, Robert Lotshaw, and Dr. E. E. Schobert for their open-mindedness and for sharing their knowledge and advice concerning primates.

Although I have not had direct contact with charitable organizations such as Primarily Primates and the International Primate Protection League, they should be recognized for their diligent work with primates that have been abandoned, neglected, or abused. An equally important aspect of their rescue work involves intervening in situations in which primate owners are not initially aware of what could be several decades of responsibility and danger, handling what are essentially wild animals, especially after they reach sexual maturity.

I want to express my gratitude to Barbara Head Millstein, for her counsel, her continued encouragement, and her belief in my work. I wish to thank David Horton for his sensitivity, editing assistance, and for opening the door to photography. I thank Merry Foresta for her insights, Christine Donnelly for her kindness, Brooks Johnson, Michael Bzdak, and Peter C. Jones for their suggestions. I thank the New Jersey State Council of the Arts fellowship for their support of this project in 1990. I want to thank Katy Homans for her beautiful book design. I am especially grateful for Jim Mairs, my editor at Norton, for his understanding and for making my photographs into a book.

The three individuals to whom the book is dedicated are my father, Paul Schwartz, who insisted on hanging my paintings of monkeys and cats in the living room, and although he never saw my photographs, somehow, I feel he would have enjoyed them; Whitey Schwartz, my cat-brother, for seventeen years of companionship, for inspiring my imagination, and for his tolerance of doll clothes and flash cubes; and my husband, Robert Forman, for urging me to continue to photograph when I said I was finished, for the endless editing decisions I asked of him, and for his sustaining love. —r. s.

Sandy, 1988. Tufted capuchin, female, 3 years old.

FOREWORD

For years I wanted a white suit after seeing Sydney Greenstreet wearing one in *Casablanca.* And I wanted a concertina after seeing Bing Crosby playing one in *True Love.* I have no idea when I first decided I had to have a monkey. Perhaps like many, I've always had a soft spot for the enchanting little creatures. For years I wanted one.

Then, in my sophomore year in college, I became the custodian of "Babinzo," a six-month-old cinnamon ringtail like Reggie, featured later in this book. With his silver face surrounded by reddish-brown hair, he looked just like a Capuchin monk with his hood up, and therefore the ringtail's more common name, "capuchin."

At nineteen there were a lot of things I didn't know, including the demanding nature of a young primate. Babinzo lived with me in our fraternity house, where he was an instant hit, beguilingly curious, clever, and cute. And mischievous as all get out. He was the equivalent of a two-year-old child with ten times the speed and energy, and a prehensile tail.

Like a young child, he needed love and affirmation. Each morning when he awoke he would jump up on my shoulder and cling with his arms around my neck, seeking security and reassurance before the day began. He didn't need much more than ten minutes, but if it was denied, because I was late for a class or for any other reason, Babinzo's day was ruined. He became petulant and retaliated with hisses, taunts, screams, bites, and did everything in his power to annoy me, stealing pencils, food, books, anything to get my attention. And although he was paper trained to a degree, he would get even by "letting fly" on a dead run. He could even do it while climbing the curtains.

Young monkeys are also sexually experimental, and Babinzo was no exception. He embarrassed me as often as possible and nearly died early when he tried to mate with a 280-pound left guard's bicep.

Without a mother's example and a forest to practice in, Babinzo's first tree experience was both pitiful and hilarious. Climbing a medium-sized maple, he leaped for what must have looked to him like another sturdy tree. The fragile shrub he landed in dropped him to the ground in a shot. He never trusted trees again.

In spite of his endearing traits, after about six months I began to feel the weight of Babinzo's needs. I wasn't ready for a commitment that could last a monkey's lifetime, thirty years or more. And much as I loved him, when I learned that friends of my parents had lost their beloved silver woolly, I offered Babinzo up for adoption. Fortunately, they accepted immediately. It is not easy to place a monkey. I would not they accepted immediately. It is not easy to place a monkey. I would not have had any regrets had Babinzo not snubbed me completely a week later, the only time I was able to visit him in his new home.

I still have the white suit, but it doesn't quite fit now. And the concertina is on a shelf in the bedroom. I never really learned how to play it.

Jim Mairs
December 1992

Ping, 1988. Capuchin, female, 5 years old.

PHOTOGRAPHER'S NOTE

I began photographing primates in captivity for this portrait series in 1987. The majority of apes and monkeys here are privately cared for, which contributes to the diversity of relationships, environments, and personal possessions seen in the photographs. I also had access to a few zoos, circuses, and other organizations. Although my project is not a nature survey, many primates are represented, including infant gorillas, chimpanzees, orangutans, gibbons, woollys, baboons, spider monkeys, various macaques and capuchins, squirrel monkeys, marmoset, lemurs, and bush babies.

When I began this project, my goal was to reveal the primates' personalities. Then, thinking of fantasy images from children's books, I tried to direct the primates, but mostly I photographed by instinct, having the flash freeze the image of my rapidly moving subjects. I usually photographed within three feet, with a 35mm lens, never through bars or Plexiglas cages. Sometimes the primates were leashed to keep them within range and protect me and the contents of the house.

As my project evolved, my primary goal became to portray the primates as individuals. I attempted to make friends so that I would be remembered on the next visit. Our interaction was essential, for without the primates' consciousness of me I would not have been able to capture the intensity of eye contact.

Although I was able to photograph many species what you see is a fictional world of primates. I sought moments and edited for photographs that do not represent the everyday world of monkeys and apes in captivity. It is not my intention in this book to encourage primate pet ownership, but to show a side of its existence, to present each primate as a unique individual, and to share my photographic fantasies.

LIKE US

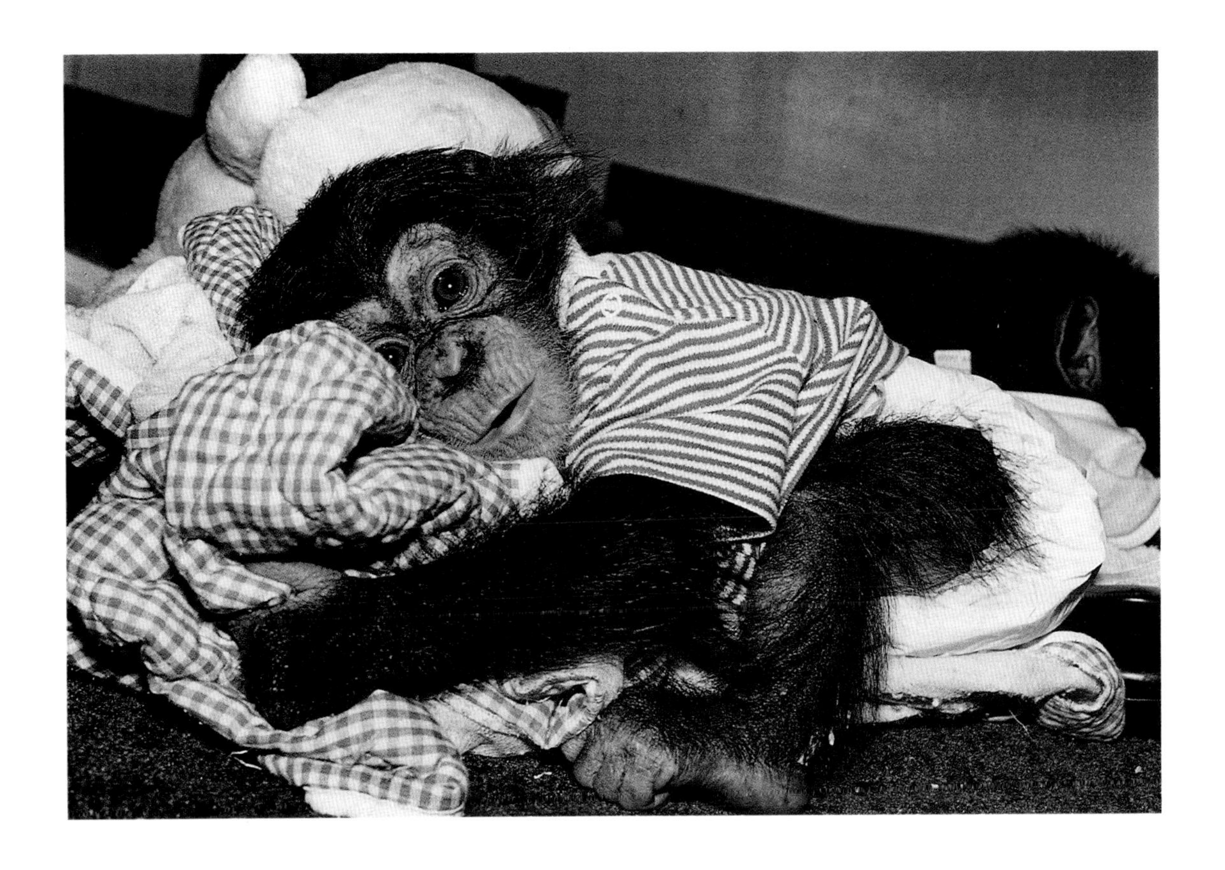

Arden, 1988. Chimpanzee, female, 5 months old.

Amy and Bridger, 1989. Black spider monkey, female, 3 years old; and Shetland sheepdog, male, 14 years old.

Teddy and Katja, 1988. Tufted capuchin, male, 3 years old; and Siamese cat, female 12½ years old.

Sweetie Pie and Cissy, 1990. Java macaques, females, 18 years and 2 years old.

Peanuts, 1990. Rhesus macaque, male, 4 years old.

Shawnee, 1990. Capuchin, female, 8 years old.

Spike, 1989. Spider monkey, male, 1 year old.

Maria, 1988. Chimpanzee, female, 2 years old.

Snuggles, 1990. Ring-tailed lemur, female, 7 weeks old.

Shibu, 1989. Crab-eating macaque, male, 18 months old.

Cissy, 1990. Java macaque, female, 2 years old.

Bubba, 1990. Gibbon, female, 4 years old.

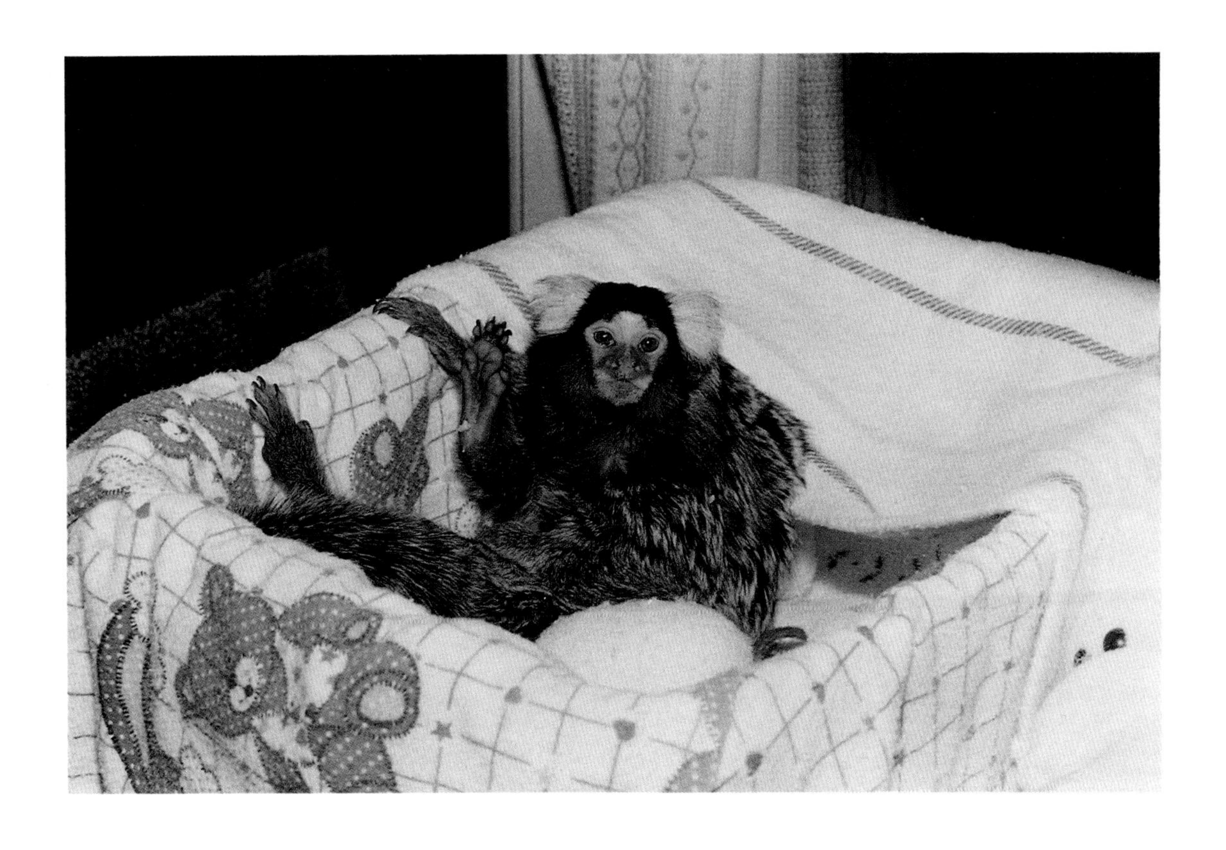

Buster, 1988. Common marmoset, male, 2 years old.

Kace, 1990. Silver spider monkey, male, 1 year old.

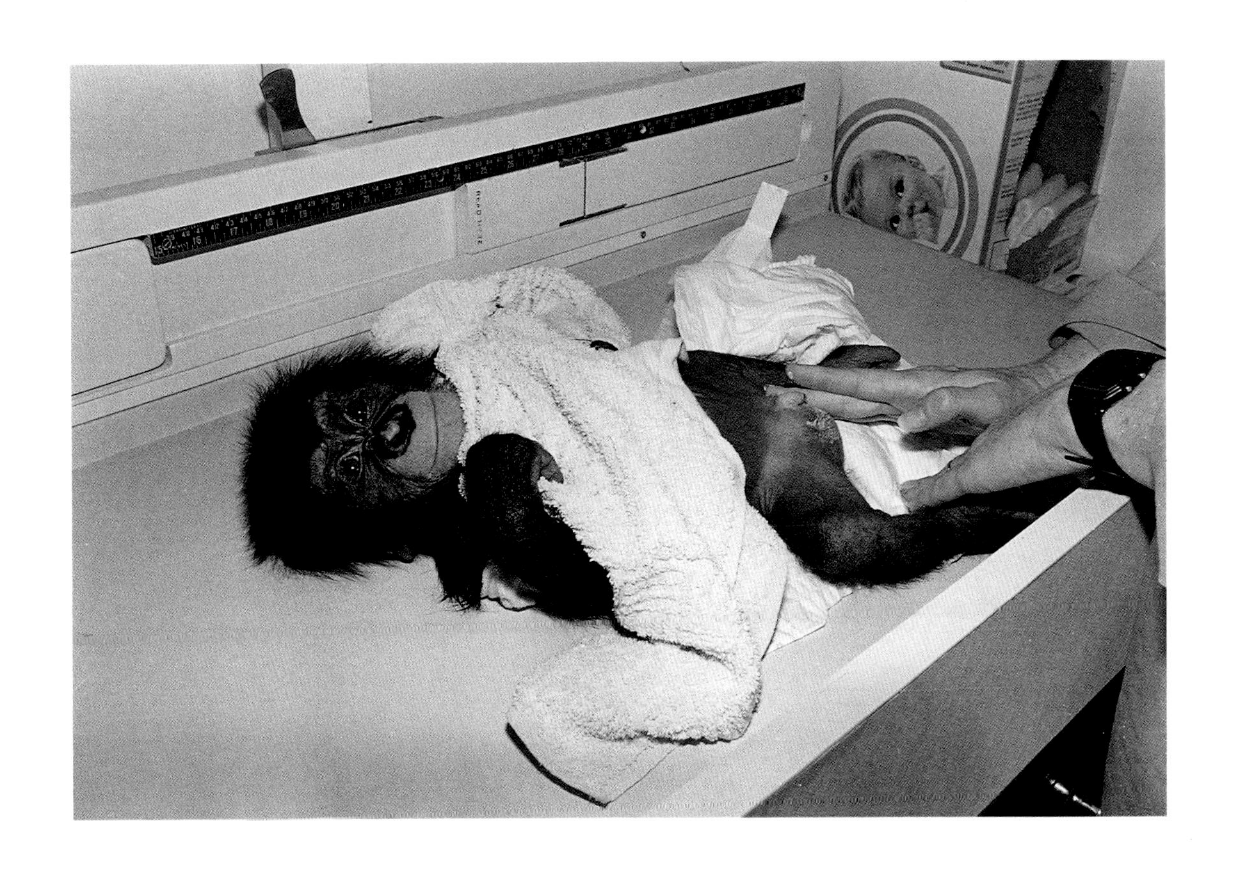

Gordo, 1988. Chimpanzee, male, 3 months old.

Congo, 1990. Celebes ape, male, 1 year old.

Elmo, Mindy, and Lindsay Ann, 1992. Spot-nosed guenon, male, 8 weeks old; capuchin, female, 8 weeks old; and girl, 3 years old.

Shibu and Peli, 1989. Crab-eating macaques: male, 18 months old; and female, 21 months old.

Penelope and Kubatzia ("Milt"), 1990. Lowland gorillas: female, 11 months old; and male, 7 months old.

Vana and Miracle, 1990. Hamadryas baboon, female, 4 years old; and toy poodle, 5 years old.

Squeaky and Happy, 1989. Squirrel monkey, male, 2 years old; and dog, female, 11 years old.

Nikko, 1990. Celebes ape, female, 5 weeks old.

Minnie, 1989. Stump-tailed macaque, female, 13 years old.

Erma, 1990. Silver spider monkey, female, age unknown.

Maretta, 1990. Mandrill baboon, female, 4 years old.

Gino and Oreo, 1990. Greater spot-nosed guenon, male, 5 years old; and potbellied pig, 1 year old.

Mikey and Jule, 1990. Celebes ape, male, 1 year old; and raccoon, female, 2 years old.

Fossie and Stone, 1992. Rhesus macaque, female, 3 years old; and Thoroughbred horse, male, 20 years old.

Julie, 1990. Orangutan, female, 4 years old.

Jake, Tabitha, and Oscar, 1990. Hamadryas baboon, male, 1 year old; English bull dog, female, 3 years old; and Siamese cat, male, 2 years old.

Jake and Tabitha, 1990. Hamadryas baboon, male, 1 year old; and English bull dog, female, 3 years old.

Melissa, 1989. Stump-tailed macaque, female, 13 years old.

Teddy, 1988. Tufted capuchin, male, 3 years old.

Sammy, 1988. Grivet guenon, male, 7 years old.

Opie, 1990. Silver spider monkey, male, 2 years old.

Wally and Spot, 1992. Squirrel monkey, male, 3½ years old; and Cornish rex kitten, male, 7 months old.

Jake and Mugs, 1990. Hamadryas baboon, male, 1 year old; and English bull dog, male, 4 years old.

Bronson, 1990. Barbary ape, male, 5 months old.

Congo, 1990. Celebes ape, male, 1 year old.

Joey and Joey's Kitty, Christine, 1989. Squirrel monkey, male, 1 year old; and cat, female, 8 months old.

Jake and Pup, 1990. Hamadryas baboon, male, 1 year old; and bull terrier.

Kiki, 1988. Orangutan, female, 2 years old.

Quincy, 1992. Bush baby, male, 1 year old.

Penelope, 1990. Lowland gorilla, female, 11 months old.

Tyson, 1992. Woolly monkey, male, 6 months old.

Freeman, 1990. Pig-tailed macaque, male, 4 years old.

Pete, 1988. Hamadryas baboon, male, 5 years old.

Squeaky and Happy, 1989. Squirrel monkey, male, 2 years old; and dog, female, 11 years old.

Reggie and Babe, 1989. Capuchin, female, 10 months old; and Shar Pei, female, 2 years old.

Libby, 1989. Stump-tailed macaque, female, 13 years old.

Libby, 1989. Stump-tailed macaque, female, 13 years old.

Junior, 1990. Celebes ape, male, 7 years old.

Charlie in the Bath, 1988. Chimpanzee, female, 5 years old.

Tarzan, 1988. White-faced capuchin, male, 18 months old.

Freeman and Gizmo, 1989. Pig-tailed macaque, male, 3 years old; and Java macaque, male, 2 years old.

Sabrina and Zandu, 1990. Pig-tailed macaque, female, 3 years old; and cat, female, 10 years old.

Bubba and pot-bellied piglet, 1990. Rhesus macaque, male, 4 years old.

Harry, 1990. Chimpanzee, male, 1 year old.

Charlie, 1988. Chimpanzee, female, 5 years old.

Peekaboo, 1990. Brown lemur, female, 1 year old.

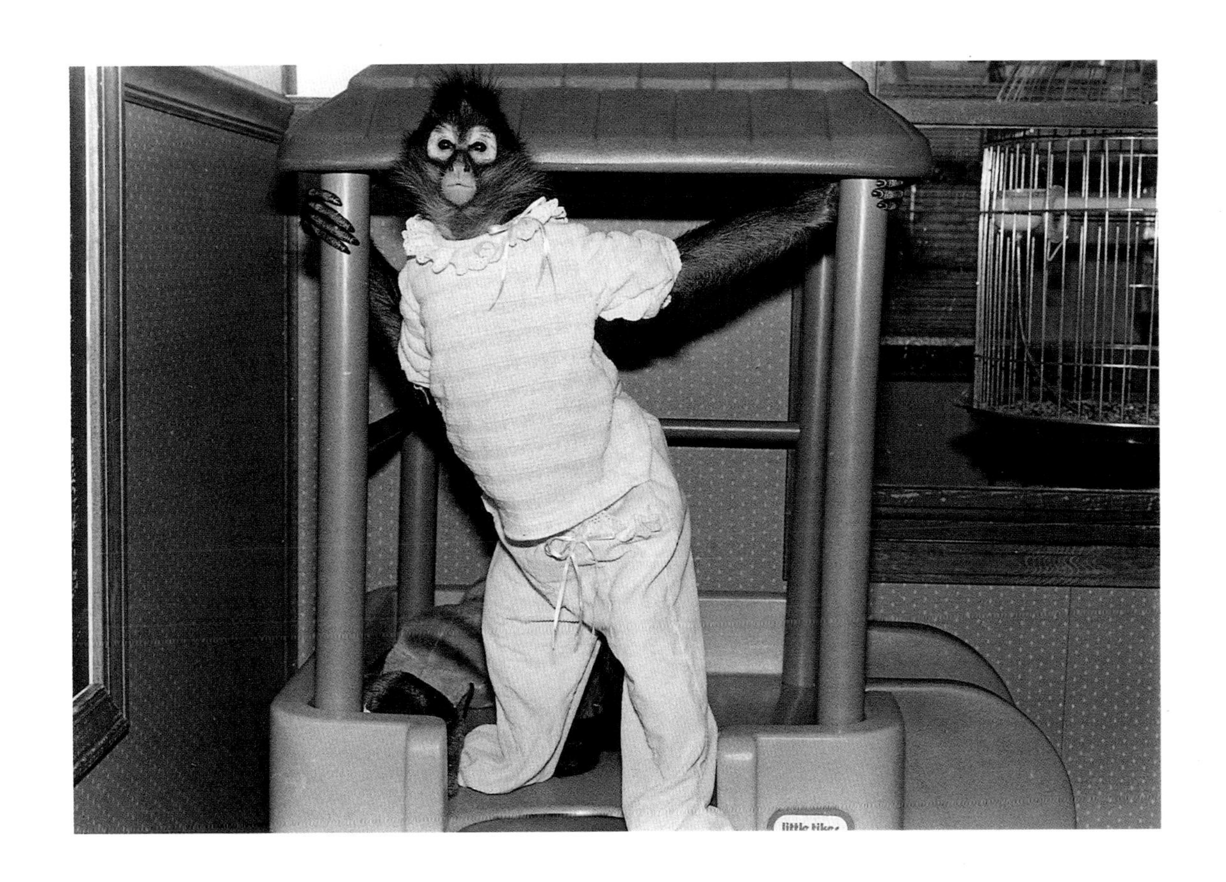

Dolly, 1990. Spider monkey, female, 4 years old.

Kubatzia ("Milt"), 1990. Lowland gorilla, male, 7 months old.

Edwina, 1988. Cinnamon capuchin, female, age unknown.

Shawnee, 1990. Capuchin, female, 8 years old.

Amy, 1989. Black spider monkey, female, 3 years old.

Chastity and Blossum, 1990. Crab-eating macaques, females, 3 years old and 4 weeks old.

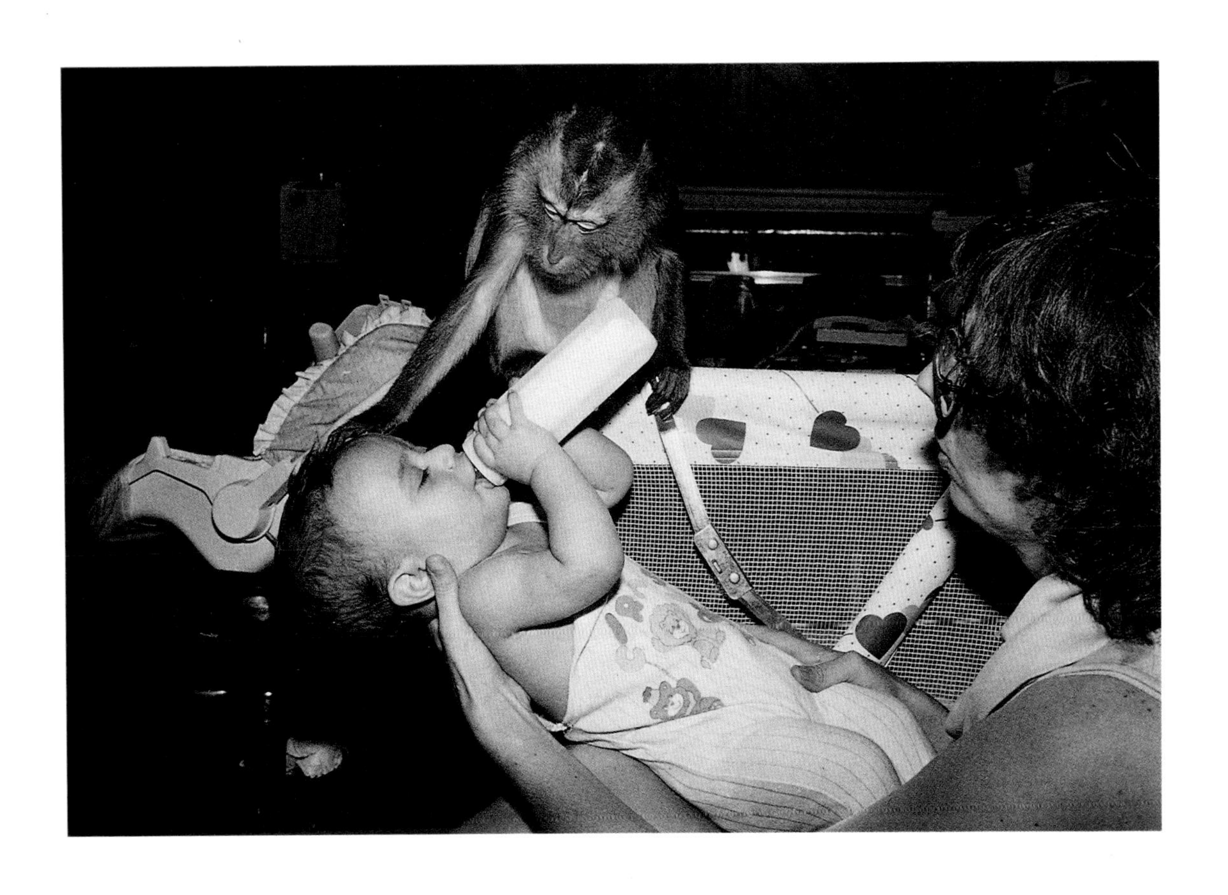

Sophie and Jeremy, 1990. Hybrid macaque, female, 4 years old: and boy, 8 months old.

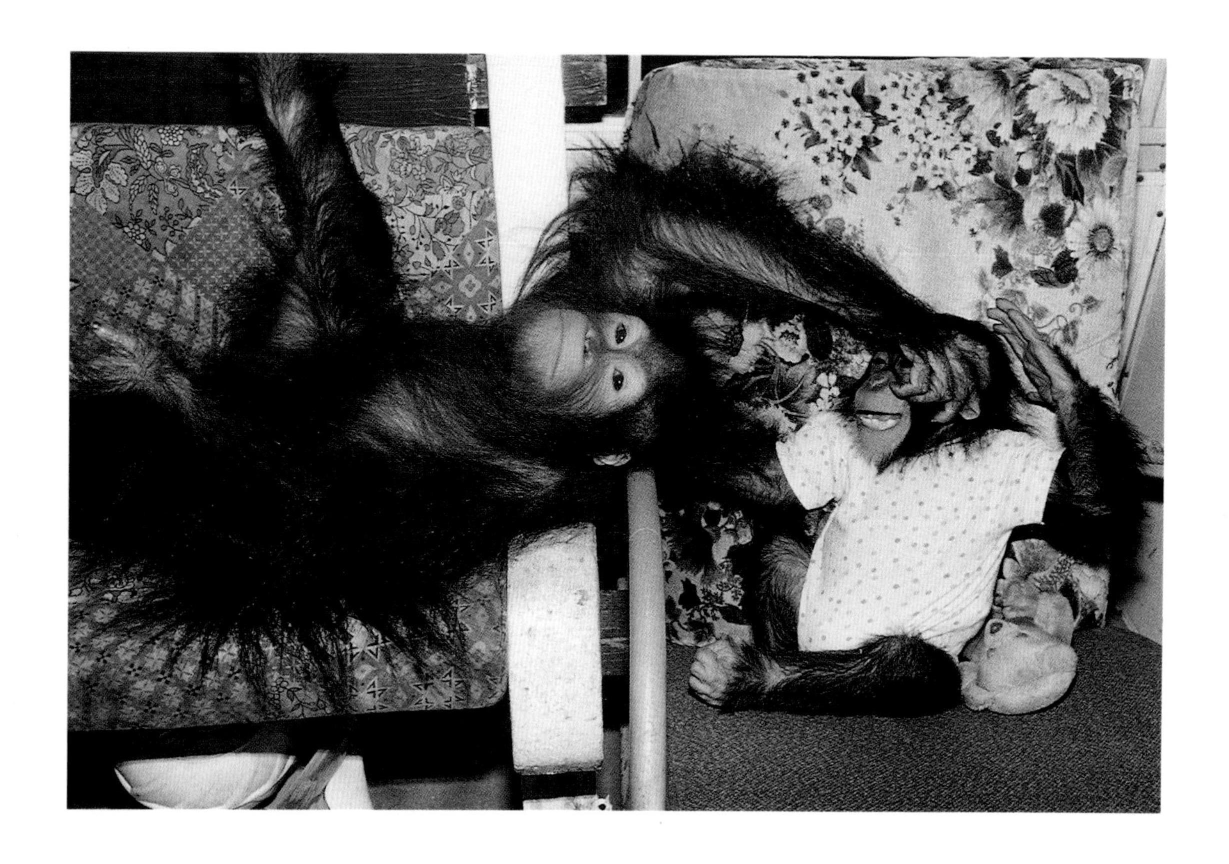

Julie and Harry, 1990. Orangutan, female, 4 years old; and chimpanzee, male, 1 year old.

Josh, Hermonie, Alexis, Rene, and Ewok, 1988. Chimpanzees, all under 1 year old.

Angel and Casey, 1989. Chimpanzees, females, 7 years old and 6 months old.

TECHNICAL NOTES

The primates were photographed within close proximity, never through bars or Plexiglas.

The cameras used were 35mm Leicas, an M4-2 and M6 with a 35mm lens. A direct flash illuminated all the primates, a Vivitar 283 flash powered by a Quantum Turbo battery pack which was charged with a quick charger.

All photographs were shot with Kodak Tri-X film developed in Rodinal and printed on Oriental Seagull paper. Prints for the book were made to size.